ALSO BY JOYCE SUTPHEN

Modern Love & Other Myths
(Red Dragonfly Press, 2015)

After Words
(Red Dragonfly Press, 2013)

House of Possibility
(Accordion Press, 2012)

First Words
(Red Dragonfly Press, 2010)

Fourteen Sonnets
(Red Dragonfly Press, 2005)

Naming the Stars
(Holy Cow! Press, 2004)

Coming Back to the Body
(Holy Cow! Press, 2000)

Straight Out of View
(Beacon Press, 1995; rpt. Holy Cow! Press, 2001)

The Green House

Joyce Sutphen

Joyce E. Sutphen (signature)

Oct 12, 2019

Published in 2017 by
Salmon Poetry
Cliffs of Moher, County Clare, Ireland
Website: www.salmonpoetry.com
Email: info@salmonpoetry.com

ISBN 978-1-910669-61-7

COVER PHOTOGRAPHY: Jessie Lendennie
COVER DESIGN & TYPESETTING: *Siobhán Hutson*
Printed in Ireland by Sprint Print

For Walt

Acknowledgments

"A Bird in County Clare," *Poetry*
"A Postcard from the Burren," *When Time and Space Conspire*, Leaning Tree Press
 "At Lissadell," *Coming Back to the Body* (out of print)
"This Beautiful Paper," "Instead," and "How I See the World," *Paper Camera*,
    New Rivers Press
"Reading the Bones," *All We Can Hold*, Sage Hill Press
"Why We Need Poetry," *Some Ride*, Weisman Art Museum
"Riding the Highway with Emily," *The Same*

Thanks to my loyal and first readers: Walt Cannon, Tim Nolan, Connie Wanek, and Phil Dentinger. I would also like to thank The Writer's Place in County Clare, Ireland, The Djerassi Foundation in California, and The Anderson Center in Red Wing, Minnesota for residencies during the time when some of these poems were written. Thanks to Gustavus Adolphus College for generous support, and to my colleagues for their ongoing encouragement and inspiration.

CONTENTS

I

II

III

I

Window

One hour or two
between the mists
from Doolin I
could see clear down
to the beach at
Lahinch. Tide's out!

Irish Suite

I. Crossing

On the way to the airport, we argue
about whether or not I should call you
when I have arrived on the other side
of the world the next day in the middle
of your night. You say, "That's what lovers do.
They call to let each other know when they're
safely there wherever it is they've gone,
and when they come back they call to say they're
on their way." "I didn't know there were rules
like that," I say. "Who made you King of Hearts?"

On the airplane, I eat the pretend food
they pretend to give me, munching fat-free
pretzels and pouring things from aluminum
into plastic. A lime wedge (slightly brown
at the edges) floats among the ice cubes.
Through the clouds, a road—no, a river!—
appears and then slips under the broad
wing just behind the lozenge of window.
After that the clouds—ice-cream castles in
the air—are blocking out the earth below.

When I am there, the wind pushes the clouds
over the high ridge. A horse, galloping,
is the one moving piece of horizon.
On the road below the window, two cars,
a blue Mercedes and a silver one,
file by (like dogs on a scent). I count shades
of green and listen to the wind pounding
against the glass. Out there, the horse is a
rock, rocking at the gate; the sea seeps through
the clouds and spreads silver across the bay.

II. At the Window

What does it mean that I am writing this
and staying in the same house the famous
poet stayed in (or, if not this one, then
one just like it, with its identical
wild-eyed cow and tufts of grass, the actual
blue inlet there, beyond the limestone hills)?
Did Emily Dickinson's fly buzz then
as it does now, flying madly around
the room while I watch the Irish cows graze
and the four horses coming through the gate?

Nothing neat, nothing too pretty about
this place; everything in casual
disarray: slates leaned up against the wall,
gold flowers between the stones in the driveway.
Even the cows across the road arrange
themselves randomly on the field as if
tossed like dice from a giant's hand.
Down to the sea, the clouds scuttle the hills,
tipping up to one side, a streak of blue
unexpectedly coming through, then sun.

On the road to Cork (and on the way back
again), we counted up years in children
and marriages. Without meaning to
I spilled a bitter story, and you told
me a thing or two in return. The car
sped through the green fields, up and down the hills
and though our hearts went open and wild, we
(neither of us) showed it on our faces.
On the road to Cork (and on the way back
again) we measured our voices in years.

III. On the Cliffs

That morning, walking on the beach between
Liscannor and Lahinch, we stepped from rock
to reach the sand and then crossed pools
until we reached the stretch of gold
and grey and black shore, sifted and swirled
together, rippled into waterless
waves that carried us East until we missed
one of the dogs and called to her despite
the wind that pushed our cries behind us as
we looked towards the graveyard of the land.

I made myself walk along the open
cliff, sick to my stomach at the closeness
of the edge, watching the opposite cliff. I
saw a man dangle over the side and turned
away, waiting for the crowd to moan when
he fell (as I felt he would), but the wind
kept up its gentle push, and the people
streamed by with their cameras. A phone rang,
and someone answered it: "Cliffs of Moher—
could you hold please? Hang on, I'll find him now."

The open sky is my comfort; over
and above me I fall into it and
let it fall into me. I ask the sky
what it is I should be forgiven for
and then I bow my head to the gravel road
pulled by thistle and vetch, stepping aside
to let the lone car pass, regaining the
way, whistling a little old-timey song.
It's the open sky I love, the way it
lifts up over the hills and cliffs like wings.

A Bird in County Clare

This morning's minion was white shouldered,
sat on the stone wall, not caught by the wind.
Slow and heavy, awkward on his thin bird
legs, he hopped sideways down the wall and stopped.

There would be no bright buckling here, no flash
of crimson gold, as the cloud and land split
open. I watched his huddled shape, feathers
blowing like the grasses in a ditch, stay

earthbound, head bowed, his dull eye turned
away from the house, his wings tucked roughly
behind his back as he noticed the complete
absence of branch and leaf, which I now saw

For the first time when I wondered what song
he might have sung, in what bare ruined choir.

A Postcard from the Burren

The quarry down the hill is deep,
its walls no different
than those of the ruined houses

we pass when we go to find
the horses: doorways gaped open,
dirt floors, the view going through

to the hillside where bushes
still yield berries, sweet
purples in the long green grass.

We do not know who lived there.
The sound of them is long gone,
echoing past Jupiter,

but the stones they stood
still stand as if to wish us here.

Moon Over Knockeven

The moon turns her half-face away
from the sea and hangs high above

the green hills. From where she is, she
can look down and see a tall house

with a black and white dog, sitting
next to the door. Behind the house,

horses; in front of it, a road
and cows. A woman is looking

out of the window of the house
watching the moon's beautiful face

high in the sky above the house,
the dog, the horses, and the cows.

County Clare Sonnet

I kept imagining the sky was blue,
that field and hedge were still within my view.

I kept seeing ocean spreading silver,
to the left, someplace that filled up nowhere.

If beyond was anywhere, it wasn't there
today, and the sky was water not air.

And then the fog lifted—not gradually,
 but as if a blanket was suddenly

snatched from the ground, exactly the way
a curtain would open to start a play,

and I could see every house from here
to the shore; I could see the hedgerows' clear

cuts between field and field. The world
returned and once more its bright leaf unfurled.

Driving the Cows, County Clare

Unlike a car, the cows
change shape as they move:

one young bull piston climbs
the back of the heifer in front of him,

front legs and hooves curved,
his wet pink mouth open in

a bellow the herd shoulders
as it does the wide cloudy sky.

Behind them, the drivers
walk, their sticks flicking

a white or golden flank,
the stream of heads, ears

tagged red, nostrils streaming,
moves past the gate and down

the lane, all hindquarters and tail.

At Clonmacnoise

As soon as we stopped the car
he was there—first
on the branch,
then the wall, and then
coming up to
the opened door, happy
to see us—it seemed—
at Clonmacnoise.

We were thinking of ships in the air,
but instead we saw
this red-breasted ruin-lover,
guardian of the marvelous, flying
against the wind
though the open arches
and roofless sanctuary
to where a monk
once knelt, praising God

for the dreams that made
him sing his songs,
turning them over
in the sweetness
of hay in the crib and milk
in the wooden bucket,
exactly the way this bird
made his given call.

One Afternoon on Highway 169

I passed a hawk stalling in the sky
above a field mouse or some

small thing of prey—it didn't matter
why he'd stopped mid-flight—what

mattered was seeing him hover there
as if he'd landed in the air, as if he hung

upon a string, a wing, until he'd
plummet down, his talon-wings wrapped

around that thing upon the ground.
I'd seen this art of treading air

once long ago in County Clare
when I was staying in a house

above Liscannor Bay (they
called that bird a kestrel there);

I looked out of the window
to catch that morning's minion

in his high riding upon the wind
and saw him hang there, hovering,

just like this hawk in Nicollet
County, just like the Windhover

in a poem by Hopkins—that soul
in parentheses and (ah!) bright wings.

Playing the Pipes

This morning in Dingle, the clouds
bellied down over the mountains
and broke into grey, white, and blue.

Winds flagged through the palm trees
that the man from the "Big House"
brought back to the bay long ago.

Up Greene Street, the school kids
in their dark uniforms gather
on the sidewalk by the Spar store.

Long ago, this was a Spanish town,
east of the Blasket Islands and west of
Connor Pass. The harbor is full of sails.

The piper sits in his little shop
on the rounding road, selling penny
whistles, telling anyone who will listen

how many ways there are
to vary the sound, how much
there is to think of all at once.

At Lissadell

We saw, from the gravel driveway, the great
windows, and, on that first visit, watched a
man and woman forage in a dumpster.

The clouds hung down over the dismal stone
as we circled the house in friendly talk.
I wondered how much of what we said

was part of a past that we only knew
because the poet made it what it was
and spoke the words that we remembered now.

We know that beauty has an enemy,
but memory summons it back from time.
They were in silk kimonos, two girls, both

beautiful. It was evening, and the light
came in the open windows; summer
was in the great green trees of Lissadel.

Inside the old Georgian mansion they talked
around the table; shadows on the wall
gathering like clouds before a storm.

Next came age and loneliness: beauty bleared
by desperate politics, the folly
of a hopeless cause and ignorant hearts.

Evening and another time: we circle
the gray bone of the past, speaking his speech,
never sure of what it is we know.

Belfast Sunday Morning

First we stop at a corner store
for newspapers—"trash mostly,"
he says; papers that we don't read

later in the upstairs restaurant
where everyone orders ciabatta
breakfasts and cappuccinos except

for me—I have poached eggs and
brown bread, and it's the best bread
I've had in years, and I would go

all the way back to Belfast for that bread
and a chance to find my way up
the hill to Queens and the bookstore

where (this time) I would buy the
boxed set of Seamus Heaney CDs
for fifty pounds without a moment's

hesitation and then up and across
on Eglantine Avenue, with a nod to
#47, and on to Lisburn Road, where

(this time) I might see Michael Longley
walking past the *Arizona* where I
am drinking cappuccino from a big

round cup and eating a perfect wedge
of pear tart clouded over with cream,
on another quiet Sunday in Belfast.

A Dream of the Future

The future that never happens
is the one that makes us do
what we do while we are waiting
for what is never going to come
to take us away from the past,
which is a country that we do not
know anymore, where the language
is strange, only almost familiar.

Years not only go by, they carry us
into places where we meet the dragons,
the gorgons, the pack of wolves
circling with their sharp teeth, and
sometimes we lift a candle, sometimes curse.
Like scarecrows, we scare a bird or two.
We know what we are and are not.

But still we keep on dreaming, warming
our hands over the fire in that cottage
at the end of the road--where everything
is prepared for us, and someone we
never met has departed only minutes ago.

Flight Home

The plane was small enough
to twist its way through the air
above the clouds packed heavy
with snow and the small bodies
of black birds.

A recorded voice told us
what we could and could not do.
We kept our seat belts on
long after we'd breached
the blue sky.

Today I saw a shadow
following a woman. It stayed
with her. It moved its legs when
she did, but it had something in
its arms—and she did not.

This is something I report
because I saw it clear and simple.
I have no explanation—nor can I
tell you how the silver plane
lifted into air.

II

This Beautiful Paper

Tonight, in an old notebook
on the reverse side of a scribbled

poem that never got off
the ground (a poem that kept

going back to the starting line
and flapping its paper wings),

I decided to be thankful for the pen
in a hand that can still hold it,

still make the ink into letters,
the letters into words that are

worlds no matter how tiny and
almost indecipherable. Tonight

I love the faint blue horizons
that cross the page, waiting

to be filled with golden light
as if in a Rembrandt painting.

Little Bee

Thought that hovers over
the open mouth of the afternoon,

useless and hapless plans
bumbling among the geraniums.

I never asked for the friends
I have; they came on the wind

and never left me. How like
a Turner sky the clouds

have made themselves—light
flaring out, edge to edge.

The Lost Alphabet

Bless all the letters that have disappeared:
the alligator, with its mouth wide open,
the band of baboons on their bikes,

the cow going over the moon, the donkey
I never saw in Dingle, the little engine that could,
the fox that stole the grapes, the horse just off

the highway in a poem by James Wright,
the lost iguana of Islington, the celebrated
jumping frog of Calaveras County,

the kite on a string over the meadow,
the nuthatch backing down a tree, the great-
horned owl and the plough-horse crossing

a field where a quail flies up and rain
comes down in sheets; bless the trampling
turtles and their uncles, the voodoo dolls of

the valley and the wildebeests of the Serengeti,
whatever is extreme, exactly who knows what:
the yak and the lost zebra in the world's last zoo.

Evening Class

The first time we met in the classroom,
the half-light in the window.

I kept subtracting words—I veered
away from "blossom" and "lovely."

Instinctively I knew
not to take on the world.

I was the mother of young children;
every week I brought home-made bread

and butter, but my poems were like
twigs on a sapling.

I had to go in another direction
in order to come close

to what he wanted to teach us,
which was always to listen

to the sound of the voice that
was ours alone, to chose

the pebble, the bird, the man
with the moon on his shoulder.

At Home

Then I knew it was true,
that I was one of them,
that we were born speaking
the same language, and that
language was our only home.

So then I knew we could be
at ease with each other,
that none of us would care
if someone broke into blossom
or stormed the blank walls.

It was good to be at home
in the world for a minute
to find myself in the
background, playing bass,
just riffing on the melody.

Snow, Snow, Snow

All the good words are gone now.
Silly to think I might say something new,

something you couldn't have said better,
letters rearranged or changed

from first thought (best)
to second (not better). I imagine

the snow-filled fields, criss-crossed
by roads and animal tracks,

and you at your desk, then
asleep on the couch,

the fire burning low
in the cast-iron stove.

How amazing that we share
this page with its deep and obscure

drifts—how right that we
might make a meeting out of snow

and resume our quiet walk through
the deep and lonely nights.

The Rhetoric of Snow

It never expects an answer.
The answer is implied

and then repeated a thousand times.
When I look up it is still coming

down, and even later, nothing has
changed. Once it has convinced

us, white is the only color we know.
Just when we begin to let go,

the sun comes back, persuading
the world into greenness,

leaving us with an emptiness
we can't begin to explain.

What It Is

Poetry is all nouns and verbs
—Marianne Moore

Then how to say "I too dislike it"
or ask "How deep is a fathom"
or say "Those are pearls
that were his eyes"?

And of my own life,
I would want to mention
the walk I took tonight
along a small lake

(I need to make that
distinction; a lake without
an adjective is larger
than I mean), where

I saw a bird, not duck
or goose or heron—
not any bird I remember
seeing before, his shoulders

hunched over as he walked
the shore, ancient as an ibis,
but (according to my bird book)
impossible in this climate.

Instead

Instead of a poem
I draw vortexes, gyring
seashells, tunnels going
in or out, depending.

I play the piano,
slow progressions
almost dissonant but
reaching towards

resolution—perhaps
and depending upon.
I wander through stores
as if racks were
islands, shelves

going fluorescent
like sunless cliffs.
Instead of a poem I
think clouds, what

holds me steady is
not expected,
when I drift and curl
like smoke in air,

circling out from
this first and last stroke
of the pen where I begin
where I end.

The Sound of a Train

Everyone imagines the poem
they would write if they were you.

They think that almost anything
that happens is good material

and that you are always waiting
for the hidden poem to appear.

They want to see you take a
coin from behind someone's ear,

they want to know the words
to the song in the distance,

The poem they imagine is better
than anything you will ever write.

The poem they imagine is so good
that you have stopped trying to write it.

Writing Poetry

First I ask them to fly.
We start by standing
on top of the desk
in the classroom, but later
we open the windows and
circle the campus, our
fingers touching the bright
tip of the chapel spire.

Next we do transformations:
water into wine, stones into
bread—the usual. Once
they've got the hang of it,
some of them like to spend
the day as various kinds of
animals and trees. At night
the astronomy class
notices constellations
that appear to be just
overhead, accompanied
by electric guitars.

The most difficult thing
we do is to sit in our chairs
very quietly and dive
deep into the ocean
in search of a pearl
(you know the one).
For now, we're building
up our lungs, seeing how
long we can stay under.

Poem Before Breakfast

So as to continue from where
last night's dream left off,

so as to think without
considering the day to come,

so as to come to the page
without final thoughts,

so as to notice the gold finches
at the feeder, the orioles

and the chickadees, so as to
remember the story your mother

told you about her only train
ride, so as to hear the train in

the distance and so feel
the ache of wanting to be

somewhere else, so as to
go back to before any of this

began—so as to begin again,
so as to continue on from here.

Even When I Write the Poem

The poem that I want to write
is stuck in my throat,
is a blur at the edge of my vision,
is a cat moving in the tall grass
behind the clothes line.

I put my body at the desk,
the fingers of my left hand
comb through my wild hair.
My feet are tapping the floor
in no particular rhythm.

The poem that I want to write
is angry, it settles scores, it explains
why we never talk anymore.
Even when I write the poem,
it doesn't make me happy.

Wandering Around the House

The words are stuck on the page; I mean
the page is stuck in words, no—what

I really mean is that I am stuck, that
something in my brain won't move

beyond the place where the words end
and the white space begins. I can't go

on so I get up and wander around
the house. The house is small, and

after a while it is like being stuck on
the page, so I go back to the words

and fill up some lines with things
I thought of when I was wandering

around the house. This lasts a few
minutes and then I arrive at the edge

of space again, pausing, wondering
what I can toss out into the empty

spot, and soon I am wandering again—
going from room to room, looking out

of every window, picking things up
and putting them down, getting a glass

out of the cupboard and opening the
refrigerator, deciding that it is time

for lunch, concentrating entirely on
toasting bread, frying bacon, slicing

tomatoes, washing lettuce, and then
slathering everything with butter

and mayonnaise, wishing you were
here to shake your head at such excess.

Why We Need Poetry

How would I know that I loved the Lions
on the steps of the Public Library

if Elizabeth Bishop hadn't called them
"agreeable" and promised they would rise

and pace through the open door up into
the reading rooms? And who would tell me

how to ride along with Death—except,
of course, Emily, who also told me

about Hope, that sturdy little thing with
feathers, singing its heart out in the storm.

When the Colonel swept the ears to the floor
and they were pressed there, listening, who would

have told their story, if not for poetry?
And how could it be the world we turn to

without knowing, unless it is our only
way to say what we feel about living

in the body? How can I learn to stand
and wait without it? Who will compare me

to a summer's day? If not for poetry,
I would not know that small birds sigh, that

butterflies sleep, that fish smile, and that words
are riprap, making a place for us to walk.

Reading the Notes in the Norton Anthology of Poetry

Some people need to be told that pullets
are chickens and that Nicollet Island

and the Guthrie are Minneapolis
landmarks. Other people (or maybe the

same ones) don't know that New Jersey is
across the Hudson from New York City's

West Side and that Stonehenge is a circle
of great standing stones on Salisbury Plain.

Some people might need to be reminded
that the Civil War ended in Eighteen-

sixty-five, and that Homer was reported
to be blind. Personally, I didn't know

that Isadora Duncan was strangled
when her scarf caught in the wheel of her car,

and I wouldn't know that a ball turret
gunner had to be a short man, though I

knew, because he "hunched in its belly" that
he looked like a fetus in a womb. And

I knew all of the words to the song in
Lowell's "Skunk Hour" and that love was "careless."

I knew too that John Keats loved Fanny Brawne,
though I'm not so sure he'd have loved kumquats.

I wish, that in addition to the things
that make up a mint julep, the editors

had given the proportions; I wish that
I could scratch the word "peat" and smell the fire

in some small cottage under Ben Bulben.
Someday I hope to hear a corncrake's cry.

For the Poet I Will Never Meet

You'd forgotten who you were
long before I started being who I am,
but when we finally met,

I liked what you had to say—
something about the world
that made it easier to take,

something that could sustain
a woman caught by the current
and swept beyond the lifeguards,

something she might say
to herself over and over
as she waited to be rescued.

Riding the Highway with Emily

She wanted to drive—
and she drove very fast,
tired of the clip-clop
of Death's carriage.

Immortality sat in back—
seated-belted and
silently screaming at
every curve.

I barely noticed the school,
but Emily saw it—and
searched for Pink Floyd
on the MP3 player,

finding, instead, The Animals
and "The House of the Rising
Sun"—which we also passed,
along with a loaded gun

and a thing with feathers.
After that, we drove for hours,
until we saw the house
with its rooftop in the ground—

I had a feeling in my bones
(like zero), but she just nodded
and drove on. Since then, we've
only stopped for a certain slant of light.

Reading the Text

What she did not say was what the words said
when you simply read them out loud, your head

making the usual calculations
with subjects and verbs. Interpretations

grew out of phantom words and lost objects
that made a pretty speech into a hex.

(Try as I might I could not hear it quite
the way she said it meant—so who was right?)

You'll have to read the poem yourself. Reader,
whoever you are, you cannot infer

what is not there unless you're into making deals
with air and wind and fire—though what appeals

to me is water. Ramon Fernadez
is just a name that Wallace Stevens liked.

The Poem Happens

The poem happens between the sound
of birds, which it finds to be
constant and not messianic.

It happens along the road
to the repeated doppler
of each passing car.

Under the pines, thick-branched towers
of green and brown, over
trunks of wooden eyes.

The poem happens in a spider's web
spun in the night and now
full of wings.

The poem happens on the shore
between waves that rub it with
watery fingers.

All the way to the cabin by the lake
the poem is making itself into
a smooth flat rock.

III

Birds of America

In the field,
in the real world of branch and sky,
I can identify so few of them.

The robin, for instance, I know by its
orange-red breast, and the chickadee
by its black cap,

and who doesn't know the large and raucous
blue jay? But in the morning
I look out at the feeder and see

birds that might be thrushes
or starlings, but clearly not
sky-larks or swallows.

What looks so discernible in a book
lifts its mysterious wings
and disappears.

I don't blame the book, the field guide
you gave me long ago. I blame
something in me that pays

too little attention, that never noticed
(until now) that you'd cut
your name off the top

of the first page, where it must have
nested once, just above
Birds of America.

The Birds Walking

I love to watch the birds walking.
Some are so contemplative:
they tuck their wings behind their backs
and gaze into the tangled earth.

Others walk in pairs, bowing to each other
as they talk about who's in and who's out.
"All the world's a cage" one says.
"I am not the golden bird" says the other.

Then a bird falls from the sky, and they disperse,
pecking at the uneven tips of green grass.
The shadows of wings ripple through the light
and over the bent backs of the birds on the ground.

I love to watch the birds walking,
to see them climb the staircase of the sky.

Herself and the Birds

Wren of a woman, her husband
a grackle, she stood at the door

of her tiny house under
the elm, welcoming us,

and curious, we went in. She
served cookies and coffee

the color of ginger ale, then
brought us to where the budgie

birds lived. We watched her
flit among them, while

her husband (the grackle)
dug in the yard. We admired

the feathered hope that sang,
we loved their velvet heads.

In August

I keep looking at the marsh as it turns
from green to gold and then loses
all its color, goes dead goes dry and is
covered up with snow. I think I am like

the marsh, am like the grasses bending down
into the wind, not like the row of birds
flying over the highway this morning
practicing it seems for lifting off

for leaving soon. I don't remember how
to go away or how to say goodbye.
I don't know who to thank or who to curse.
I keep looking at the marsh as it turns

from green to gold and then loses
all its color, goes dead goes dry and is
covered up with snow. I think I am like
the marsh—I think I am like the marsh.

The Crows

All afternoon, they fly over the trees
at the edge of the marsh, filling the sky

with their caws, answering each other in
code. I look for the owl, but cannot find

him, get distracted by an article
about Oscar Wilde—I've always been fond

of Oscar—and by the time I finish
reading about Dorian Gray, the crows

have moved away, most likely to a small
hotel in Chelsea, just down the road from

Bob and Peggy's flat in Lennox Gardens.
Poor Oscar, I thought of him in Paris.

Today the crows return, glossy and sleek
as nineteenth century men in frock coats.

The Cardinal

The cardinal who crashed
into my window
is lying on the patio
like a blossom fallen from
an Amaryllis in January.

His tiny feet are pointed
to the sky; he is so lately dead
it seems that he could fly,
except that his eyes are shut
above his mask; his wings

are neatly tucked, and his
head rests on its broken stem.
He is so lovely lying there
I do not want to move him,
but later, before the coyotes

come, I will carry him to
the marsh and fling him out—
along with branches from
the storm, a raku cup, and
a gold ring I'll never wear again.

Amaryllis

Who will tell of the amaryllis
now that long weeks later
through dark December nights

and up the green stalk
of the New year, the crowned
head is opening

the way a beautiful woman
unbuttons her coat and steps out
in a red dress?

And who will tell
how each petal overlaps
and repeats the striped pattern

as the flower bends, bends to open
while behind it another
head nods and unfurls

its trumpet of light,
the clear call of it
filling the room.

Hawk and Fields

Just as I drove by,
the hawk landed
on a telephone pole,

and then I passed
the soybean fields,
yellow as the gold

in a Van Gogh painting
or the rapeseed fields
on the way to Dover.

When I was a child,
I thought the only yellow
fields were made of oats.

I thought the hawk
was a circle, high
in a cloudy sky.

The Mouth of Language

Not in the sense of speaking—
of putting thought into words,
or wrapping sense in sound,
but as in the mouth of a mother cat,
carrying her mewling kittens
into the yellow light of the barn.

And not as in the jaw and teeth,
the tongue and lips that give
to airy nothing a voice,
but as in river flowing into
ocean, as in silt and sand and clay,
as solid as the land, as bright as day.

Not the proclamation, not the edict—
just the mumble, hum, and sigh, singing
the tune without the words.

Grammar Lessons

I used to like making diagrams of sentences
I was never going to say: Yes, I will marry
you. No, I only want to live forever.

I could lay it out on paper: subject
and verb, not to mention direct object
and the prepositional phrases I never ended

with—if I could help it, but I couldn't.
I wrote between the lines; I wrote
outside the margins; I caused a rift somewhere

in deepest deep down structure. So after that
it was all stream of consciousness—no need for
reasonable thinking, straight or not; I shot

the bolt, I spent it all on adjectives
and verbs until I learned how much I loved
the nouns: tree, bird, stone, and cradle.

Still Life

On the desk, brocaded cloth and
a brass lamp. Numbers in columns and
a scattering of pens. Keys on a ring.

Remember the way time used to fly
with calendar wings? The years
went by like shuffled cards, a flip

book that made the cat play a jig
on his fiddle and the cow jump over
the moon. How mysterious.

I do not think I am afraid to die.
I think that dying does not frighten me.
I am not thinking about being dead.

Just when I thought the poem was
over I heard a train in the distance,
and now a car is climbing the road.

The Soul

When I was a child,
I was taught that I *had* a soul—
not that I had soul.

My soul lived inside the temple
of the body like a bird
in a cage—a ghostly white

shape that glowed in the dark
like the phosphorescent rosary
on my grandmother's night table.

It was important to keep my soul
spotless, so that God would want
to live there . . . or was that my heart

he would come to visit one day,
knocking until I opened the door?

Observation Point

Look until you see
what you did not
see at first.
Listen
at the same time.

Don't let the breeze
go unnoticed.
How many words
do you know for
the way things smell?

What do you call that
sense that feels the clear
blue space between one
tree and the next?
What bird is that, singing

far out in the marsh?
Can you eat those berries,
ripening all around you?
(the ones you took so long
to notice).

Constable Clouds

How is it that the sky looks more
like a painting than the painting

looks like the sky? How does that
maple do color—as if a brush

dipped in orange had swept over
it as it passed, leaving just

that blush of orange on the green?
How is air thinner than the distance

between things? How is depth
deeper when you look away

and back again?   How is it possible
that this moment (leaves falling

from the maples, blackbirds)
is shorter than eternity?

Bird Song, Cannon River Bottoms

I stopped for the sound,
thinking of the end of Keats's ode,
"To Autumn."

The cars on the distant road
replaced the lamb's loud bleat,
and bicyclists went whirling by.

Then choruses
of trills and twitterings
filled the stadium of the air—

then faded away
as quickly as they came.
Two men on roller blades went by,

a siren wailed.
I heard the sound of wings
. . . and slowly it started up again—

a tweet, a chirp,
a long sentence in a language
that may have been lark.

We Shadows

Climbed slowly to the top—
of what? We were not sure,

but to us it meant that
we could look down

in every direction; it meant
we had reached the summit

and having stood there
long and quietly, waiting

for the god—in whatever shape
he chose to appear—we

shrugged and said it was not
the day for revelations,

that we could come again,
and that someday—when

we least expected it—we'd
meet her—how? and who

knows when? And as we
descended, we watched

our shadows—beautiful
and dark against the cliffs.

Posing

When you see my face again,
now (how I am, all these years
later) you'll see that I am still

looking at you, looking like myself,
wondering what it is you'll see
when, in the moment, I'm caught.

Of all the days since I last saw you,
only this one is snapped, shot,
no space anywhere to say

what I would never say to you
in person. This is a photograph
from a real life, not a movie.

I look at the camera, steady on,
as if I did not know that you would
see me still looking at you.

Burne-Jones: The Golden Stairs

They are all the same woman:
she is
looking down,

looking back,
looking pensive.
She is

holding a trumpet,
holding a harp,
holding her breath,

as she
steps forward,
steps down,

stands still
on the stairs, in a dress
tied with a scarf

at the waist,
below her breasts, or
wrapped around her shoulders,

and her hair is
pulled back,
pinned up,

plaited with leaves,
and her feet are all bare,
and her lips are all closed,

and everywhere she is
there are more
        of her,

and everywhere
she looks
she sees only herself.

The Photo Album

I must conclude, from the photos, that I
was bored with happiness, that I found it
tedious to endure so many days
of ordinary domestic bless. This,
I say, may be the case, or else I may
have felt nothing of what those pictures seem
to show. I know that the shutter opens
and closes on a moment's face, and what
is there to do but smile when one is asked?
I have. I did. I smiled when I was bid.

I notice how we spent summers: building
sandcastles, diving from the dock, going
in and out the waters. I see how far
away I am in the next pictures, almost
invisible, fading into distant
buildings in foreign cities. In the box
of photographs everything happens
at once: the daughters grow up and put on
makeup; they go to proms and graduate
from high school. They pose with forgotten boys.

And now I wonder what kept us going
all those years of black and white, those soundless
and still days when things we wanted to say
were written down: ink on paper, something
that arrived one morning and seemed to know
what we were about to do, mysterious
as the faces in the photographs—those
faces we hadn't yet met: our children
and their children's children's children, smiling—
all of them—into the future's bright flash.

Reading the Bones

What have I been doing long enough so
that my skeleton would tell you who I
am? Is the way I'm holding this pen
worn into the thumb and the finger bones

of my hand? Is there evidence that I once
fell from a roof? That a tractor wheel went
over my leg or that a dog's teeth went
into my arm? Will someone say: "Woman,

carried a child on her hip, rocked babies
in her arms, pushed a grocery cart down
florescent aisles at midnight counting dimes,
Had no idea that love could be a noun.

Whatever they find from reading the bones,
They'll never know how amazing it was.

Eclipses

Remember Romeo and Rosamond?
Then came Juliet. Romeo and Juliet!

The way that Elvis eclipsed
that other guy—what was

his name? You can't
remember now.

The way the hamburger
eclipsed bologna and white bread,

and chocolate cake eclipsed
everything else on the menu,

or remember how the wash line
was eclipsed by a machine

imitating wind
and the heat of the sun?

Horses pulling a plow,
eclipsed by a tractor

and then a mountain of steel
on giant wheels,

and remember love—
how it eclipsed everything?

Independence Day

I pledge allegiance to the clouds
moving across the sky,
changing from camel to whale,

to the wind that fills the trees,
lifts the curtain, and
is gone,

to voices across the meadow, the air
in pieces, to the dog barking
from the corner of a hill,

to birds whose names I've never known,
to their familiar affable bodies
hidden in the tops of trees,

to the man driving his car along the freeway,
watching buildings and billboards
approach and disappear,

to the bones inside our bodies, netted through
with tendons and veins,
to how they hold us up—to bones!

and to touching skin on skin, to fingertips
lips on breasts and thigh rubbing thigh,
to love, again and again.

Good

I'm good at being where
I should be when I shouldn't be,

at saying the almost right
thing at exactly the wrong

time. I'm good at indecision,
good at leaving just as the

blizzard is about to begin,
finally selling that piece

of land as the market crashes.
I'm good at spider webs and

finding tiny agates; if you
lost something I'm good at

finding it where you've already
looked twenty times before.

I'm good at forgetting,
forgiving everything that

happened, happy just to sit
with you watching clouds—

I've always been good at
watching clouds and listening

to you talk, so just keep talking
and I'll listen. I'm good at that.

How I See the World

In color, just like I dream, and always
gratefully, though perhaps I often seem
distracted. (I am, aren't you?)

I see it in voices coming to me
on the radio, in the telephone,
and on the wind. I hear it in the words

I read on the page, I see it in time—
one of us being born and the other
dying. Spring and Fall—both at once.

Death. Whatever that is. I can't see it,
but how I love the way that leaf (just now
when I looked up) floated down from the tree

so slowly, taking its time—all the time
in the world—for me to see it falling.

The Cup

Yesterday, in the café,
how beautiful the cup

that held your tea—
the yellow tea in the

clear glass, and the flowers
in the shimmering pouch,

and how well you told
the stories that fit

into the hour (which
lasted exactly as long

as a cup of tea) in the
clear blue tint of the glass

and how . . . "comfortable"
(I thought) I've always

felt with you. Even in
the rain, which you

promised would come,
I'm remembering

the cup—how beautiful
the cup—in the yellow café.

JOYCE SUTPHEN grew up on a farm in Stearns County, Minnesota. Her first collection of poems, *Straight Out of View*, won the Barnard New Women Poets Prize; *Coming Back to the Body* was a finalist for a Minnesota Book Award, and *Naming the Stars* won a Minnesota Book Award in Poetry. In 2005, Red Dragonfly Press published Fourteen Sonnets in a letterpress edition. She is one of the co-editors of *To Sing Along the Way*, an award winning anthology of Minnesota women poets. Her fourth collection, *First Words*, was published in 2010; in 2012, *House of Possibility*, a letter press edition of poems, was published by Accordion Press, followed by *After Words*, which was published in 2013, and *Modern Love & Other Myths* (2015), which was a finalist for a Minnesota Book Award. She is the second Minnesota Poet Laureate, succeeding Robert Bly, and she teaches literature and creative writing at Gustavus Adolphus College in St. Peter, Minnesota.